Schitt's Creek
Unofficial Cookbook

The Taste & Easy Recipes Inspired by Schitt's Creek

Tammy Bowley

© Copyright 2021 - All rights reserved.

The content contained within this book may not be reproduced, duplicated or transmitted without direct written permission from the author or the publisher.

Under no circumstances will any blame or legal responsibility be held against the publisher, or author, for any damages, reparation, or monetary loss due to the information contained within this book, either directly or indirectly.

Legal Notice:

This book is copyright protected. It is only for personal use. You cannot amend, distribute, sell, use, quote or paraphrase any part, or the content within this book, without the consent of the author or publisher.

Disclaimer Notice:

Please note the information contained within this document is for educational and entertainment purposes only. All effort has been executed to present accurate, up to date, reliable, complete information. No warranties of any kind are declared or implied. Readers acknowledge that the author is not engaged in the rendering of legal, financial, medical or professional advice. The content within this book has been derived from various sources. Please consult a licensed professional before attempting any techniques outlined in this book.

By reading this document, the reader agrees that under no circumstances is the author responsible for any losses, direct or indirect, that are incurred as a result of the use of the information contained within this document, including, but not limited to, errors, omissions, or inaccuracies.

Table of Contents

Introduction 5

Breakfast Recipes 7

    Johnny Rose Apricot Bars 7

    Moira Rose Apple Muffins 9

    David Rose Creamy Banana Oatmeal 11

    Alexis Rose Banana Nut Porridge 13

    Jocelyn Schitt Chestnut Flour Crepes 15

    Mutt Schitt Breakfast Sausage 17

    Stevie Budd Sausage Frittata 19

    Roland Schitt Coconut Porridge 21

Smoothie Recipes 23

    Robert Currie Banana Avocado Smoothie 23

    Twyla Sands Coconut Peach Smoothie 25

    Veronica Lee Bacon Chocolate Smoothie 27

    Theodore Mullens Pumpkin Smoothie 29

    Patrick Brewer Banana Coconut Smoothie 31

    Johnny Rose Apple Smoothie 33

    Moira Rose Strawberry-Raspberry Smoothie 35

    David Rose Guava Papaya Smoothie 37

Chicken Recipes 38

    Alexis Rose Bacon Wrapped Chicken Tenders 38

    Jocelyn Schitt African Style Chicken Stew 40

Mutt Schitt Roasted Dried Herb Drumsticks 42

Stevie Budd Pineapple Citrus Marinated Chicken 44

Roland Schitt BBQ Chicken Drumsticks 46

Twyla Sands Basil Pesto Chicken 48

Robert Currie Roasted Chicken Thighs 50

Veronica Lee Chicken Piccata 52

Snacks Recipes 54

Theodore Mullens Roasted Peanuts 54

Johnny Rose Cheddar Biscuits 58

Moira Rose Spicy Cashews 60

David Rose Chickpea Crackers 62

Alexis Rose Herb Crackers 64

Jocelyn Schitt Lemon Scones 66

Mutt Schitt Banana Biscuits 68

Dessert Recipes 70

Stevie Budd Blueberry Ice-cream 70

Roland Schitt Chickpea Fudge 72

Twyla Sands Blackberry Crumble 74

Robert Currie Chocolate Mousse 76

Veronica Lee Banana Custard 78

Theodore Mullens Blueberry Pudding 80

Patrick Brewer Chocolate Custard 82

Johnny Rose Mint Chocolate Chip Ice-cream 84

Conclusion 86

Introduction

In today's hectic world where everyone is in a rush, with depression and anxiety blooming around, the best remedy to feel the blessing of life is a comedy to lighten the environment and food to cherish the joy. There is so much in life to be happy about, and comedy is the best way to ease down the tensed atmosphere and burdens of work. The combination of food and humor together is, without a doubt, the most effective therapy which can make not only you but your surroundings cheered up and fade of all the blues of life.

To give this idea a proper shape, "Schitt's Creek Unofficial Cookbook" comes in. It is Inspired by the comedy TV show Schitt's Creek. The book came out as a direct inspiration from the show where you can pay your honor and gratitude to the picturesqueness in Emlade County. The show offers various recipes for almost every occasion and everyone without neglecting anybody at all/. It genuinely does not actually matter if you are into homemade food in your kitchen or an outside diner at cafes and restaurants. The book has to offer everybody with delicious and finger-licking recipes all inspired by one of the greatest humor TV series of recent times, i.e., Schitt's Creek.

The recipes involve special meals from Jocelyn's humble & down to earth meals, recipes from the Rosebud Motel, and special dishes form Café Tropical. Furthermore, all the recipes are thoroughly revised, written profoundly and provides the ultimate convenience with step by step instruction. To add more, the recipes are prepared from the healthiest and nutritious ingredients because we care about your wellbeing and you being happy and healthy. After all, laughers and good food are what we always will strive for deep-down as humans.

The book offers a total of 40+ dishes, comprising drinks & beverages, desserts, appetizers, entrees, and much more. The recipes are very convenient to make, and you quickly cook them while watching your favorite TV show to actually feel your food the most. The book is thoroughly devised into chapters, and with every passing chapter, you will see colorful and nutritious ingredients being used in finger-licking and delicious recipes that are totally inspired form your favorite characters from Schitt's Creek. It is just not restricted to cheese only; it comes with a lot of recipes like Sloppy Jocelyn's, There's a Dead Guy in Room 4-Cheese Macaroni, Rosebud Motel Cinnamon Rolls, Twyla's Meadow Harvest Smoothie, Herb Ertlinger's Wine Spritzer, Farm Witches' Peanut Butter Things, Budd's Bourbon BBQ Sauce, and much more.

The book offers recipes for every chef, considering the difficulty level. The overall difficulty level increases as you go further through the book. But certainly, you don't have to worry about it as the recipes include easily scripted instructions with every step explained thoroughly, minimizing any doubts or ambiguities at all. Clearly, it means that you can go through baking, cooking, and eating the most delicious meals with the Schitt's Creek Unofficial Cookbook. All you need to do is simply put on an apron. Heat up your oven, play your favorite episode from Schitt's Creek, and start cooking with Schitt's Creek Unofficial Cookbook.

Breakfast Recipes

Johnny Rose Apricot Bars

Preparation Time: 7 minutes
Cooking Time: 25 minutes

Servings: 2

Ingredients:

- ½ cup dried apricots
- ¼ cups chocolate chips

- 1 cup pecans
- ½ tablespoon vanilla extract
- 1 large egg
- Salt, to taste

Preparation:

1. Preheat the oven to 350 degrees F.
2. Meanwhile, put apricots and pecans in a blender and blend well.
3. Now, add in egg, vanilla essence, and salt. Blend until a smooth mixture is formed.
4. Take out and fold in chocolate chips.
5. Transfer the mixture in a greased baking dish and bake for about 25 minutes.
6. Take out and cut into slices.
7. Serve and enjoy!

Serving Suggestions: Pour chocolate syrup on the apricot bars before serving.

Variation Tip: You can also use white chocolate chips.

Nutritional Information per Serving:

Calories: 225 | **Fat:** 14g|**Sat Fat:** 5.7g|**Carbohydrates:** 18.3g|**Fiber:** 2.2g|**Sugar:** 15.2g|**Protein:** 6g

Moira Rose Apple Muffins

Preparation Time: 5 minutes
Cooking Time: 20 minutes

Servings: 2

Ingredients:

- 1 cup almond flour
- 2 eggs
- ½ teaspoon baking soda
- 1 apple, chopped
- 1 teaspoon ground cinnamon
- 1 tablespoon melted butter
- 1 tablespoon honey
- Salt, to taste

Preparation:

1. Preheat the oven to 350 degrees F.
2. Meanwhile, add eggs, almond flour, honey, baking soda, chopped apple, ground cinnamon, butter, and salt in a bowl. Beat well.
3. When the mixture becomes smooth, pour it in the muffin cups and place them in the baking oven.
4. Bake for about 20 minutes and take out.
5. Serve and enjoy!

Serving Suggestions: Top it with apple syrup before serving.

Variation Tip: You can use coconut flour instead of almond flour.

Nutritional Information per Serving:

Calories: 543 | **Fat:** 36.9g|**Sat Fat:** 7g|**Carbohydrates:** 37.3g|**Fiber:** 9.3g|**Sugar:** 20.6g|**Protein:** 18g

David Rose Creamy Banana Oatmeal

Preparation Time: 10 minutes
Cooking Time: 5 minutes

Servings: 2

Ingredients:

- 2 bananas
- ½ teaspoon ground cinnamon powder
- 4 tablespoons coconut butter
- Salt, to taste

Preparation:

1. Put bananas in a bowl and mash well with a fork.
2. Add in salt and cinnamon and mix well.
3. Meanwhile, heat coconut butter in a saucepan.
4. Add banana mixture in the saucepan and cook over low flame.
5. Take out, serve, and enjoy!

Serving Suggestions: Serve with the topping of banana slices and honey.

Variation Tip: Almond butter can also be used.

Nutritional Information per Serving:

Calories: 291 | **Fat:** 18.4g|**Sat Fat:** 16.1g|**Carbohydrates:** 34g|**Fiber:** 8.1g|**Sugar:** 16.3g|**Protein:** 3.3g

Alexis Rose Banana Nut Porridge

Preparation Time: 10 minutes
Cooking Time: 5 minutes

Servings: 8

Ingredients:

- 1 cup raw pecans
- 1 cup raw cashews
- 1 cup raw almonds
- 2 bananas
- 4 teaspoons cinnamon
- 4 cups coconut milk
- Salt, to taste

Preparation:

1. Add nuts and salt in a bowl and soak them in water overnight.
2. Rinse the nuts and place them in a food processor.
3. Add bananas, coconut milk, and cinnamon in the food processor. Pulse well.
4. After that, transfer the mixture in the saucepan and cook for about 5 minutes over medium-high heat.
5. Take out and serve.

Serving Suggestions: Top with banana slices and nuts before serving.

Variation Tip: You can use almond milk instead of coconut milk.

Nutritional Information per Serving:

Calories: 484 | **Fat:** 43.9g|**Sat Fat:** 27.6|**Carbohydrates:** 22.7g|**Fiber:** 6.2g|**Sugar:** 9.1g|**Protein:** 8.4g

Jocelyn Schitt Chestnut Flour Crepes

Preparation Time: 5 minutes
Cooking Time: 7 minutes

Servings: 4

Ingredients:

- 1 cup chestnut flour
- 1 egg
- ½ cup coconut milk
- ½ cup water
- ½ tablespoon coconut oil

Preparation:

1. In a blender, add egg, water, and milk. Blend well.
2. Now, add in chestnut flour and coconut oil. Blend until a smooth mixture is formed.
3. Grease a skillet and pour the batter in it.
4. Cook for about 2 minutes on each side and take out.
5. Serve and enjoy!

Serving Suggestions: Serve with some honey and cream.

Variation Tip: Use unsweetened coconut milk.

Nutritional Information per Serving:

Calories: 192 | **Fat:** 10.9g|**Sat Fat:** 8.3g|**Carbohydrates:** 21.2g|**Fiber:** 3g|**Sugar:** 1.1g|**Protein:** 3.7g

Mutt Schitt Breakfast Sausage

Preparation Time: 10 minutes
Cooking Time: 15 minutes

Servings: 2

Ingredients:

- ¼ teaspoon cayenne
- ½ teaspoon fresh grated nutmeg
- ½ pound ground beef
- ½ pound ground pork
- ½ pound ground bison
- ½ teaspoon black pepper
- 1 teaspoon fresh thyme, chopped
- 1 teaspoon fresh sage, chopped
- ½ teaspoon fresh rosemary, chopped
- Salt, to taste

Preparation:

1. Add cayenne, nutmeg, ground beef, ground pork, ground bison, black pepper, thyme, sage, salt, and rosemary in a bowl and mix well.
2. Make 2 inch balls and place them in a plate.
3. Meanwhile, grease a skillet and place it over medium-low heat.
4. Add sausages in it and sauté for about 15 minutes.
5. Take out and serve.

Serving Suggestions: Serve with garlic sauce.

Variation Tip: Oregano can be added to enhance taste.

Nutritional Information per Serving:

Calories: 651 | **Fat:** 28.6g|**Sat Fat:** 11.6g|**Carbohydrates:** 1.5g|**Fiber:** 0.8g|**Sugar:** 0.2g|**Protein:** 91.3g

Stevie Budd Sausage Frittata

Preparation Time: 5 minutes
Cooking Time: 10 minutes

Servings: 2

Ingredients:

- ½ sweet potato, peeled and grated
- 5 eggs
- 2 green onions, diced
- 1½ tablespoons coconut oil
- 2 cups crumbled sausages
- Pepper, to taste

Preparation:

1. Add coconut oil in a skillet and place it over medium heat.
2. Add crumbled sausages in the skillet and sauté until golden brown.
3. Add in grated sweet potato and cook until tender.
4. Now, add onions and cook for 2 to 3 minutes.
5. Add beaten eggs on the sausage mixture and cook for about 3 minutes.
6. Now, transfer the mixture in the broiler and broil on low heat until completely cooked.
7. Take out and serve.

Serving Suggestions: You can serve the frittata with bread.

Variation Tip: You can also use tomatoes to enhance taste.

Nutritional Information per Serving:

Calories: 554 | **Fat:** 52.1g|**Sat Fat:** 37g|**Carbohydrates:** 7.9g|**Fiber:** 1.4g|**Sugar:** 3.1g|**Protein:** 17.2g

Roland Schitt Coconut Porridge

Preparation Time: 10 minutes
Cooking Time: 10 minutes

Servings: 12

Ingredients:

- ½ cup coconut milk
- ½ tablespoon golden flaxseed meal
- ½ cup shredded organic coconut
- 1 tablespoon almond flour
- ½ teaspoon vanilla essence

- 1 tablespoon honey
- Salt, to taste

Preparation:

1. Add milk in a saucepan and heat it.
2. Now, add vanilla essence, honey, salt, almond flour, shredded coconut, and golden flaxseed meal in the pan. Mix well.
3. Let the mixture simmer over medium-heat until the mixture becomes thick.
4. Take out and serve.

Serving Suggestions: Serve with some nuts.

Variation Tip: You can replace coconut milk instead of almond milk.

Nutritional Information per Serving:

Calories: 45 | **Fat:** 3.9g|**Sat Fat:** 3.1g|**Carbohydrates:** 2.7g|**Fiber:** 0.7g|**Sugar:** 2g|**Protein:** 0.5g

Smoothie Recipes

Robert Currie Banana Avocado Smoothie

Preparation Time: 10 minutes

Servings: 4

Ingredients:

- 2 avocados, pitted
- 1 cup water
- 2 bananas

- 1 cup spinach

Preparation:

1. Add avocados, bananas, water, and spinach in a food processor.
2. Pulse until a smooth mixture is formed.
3. Take out and serve with a smile.

Serving Suggestions: Top with mint leaves before serving.

Variation Tip: You can also add crushed ice.

Nutritional Information per Serving:

Calories: 259 | **Fat:** 19.8g|**Sat Fat:** 4.2g|**Carbohydrates:** 22.4g|**Fiber:** 8.4g|**Sugar:** 7.8g|**Protein:** 2.8g

Twyla Sands Coconut Peach Smoothie

Preparation Time: 10 minutes
Servings: 4

Ingredients:

- 4 peaches, peeled and chopped
- 2 cups coconut milk, chilled
- 2 cups ice
- Lemon zest, to taste

Preparation:

1. Add peaches, coconut milk, lemon zest, and ice in a blender.
2. Blend until a smooth mixture is formed.
3. Take out and pour into serving glasses.
4. Serve and enjoy!

Serving Suggestions: Top it with mint leaves.

Variation Tip: Almond milk can also be used.

Nutritional Information per Serving:

Calories: 339 | **Fat:** 29.1g | **Sat Fat:** 25.4g | **Carbohydrates:** 22g | **Fiber:** 5.4g | **Sugar:** 18.4g | **Protein:** 4.3g

Veronica Lee Bacon Chocolate Smoothie

Preparation Time: 10 minutes

Servings: 8

Ingredients:

- 4 cups coconut milk
- 4 tablespoons cocoa powder
- 8 strips of cooked regular bacon
- 1 cup ice cubes
- 4 tablespoons maple syrup

Preparation:

1. Add coconut milk, cocoa powder, and maple syrup in a blender. Blend well.
2. Now, add bacon strips and ice cube and blend until a smooth mixture is formed.
3. Take out and serve with a smile.

Serving Suggestions: Top with some chocolate chips before serving.

Variation Tip: You can use honey instead of maple syrup.

Nutritional Information per Serving:

Calories: 321 | **Fat:** 30g|**Sat Fat:** 25.9g|**Carbohydrates:** 14.9g|**Fiber:** 3.4g|**Sugar:** 10g|**Protein:** 4.1g

Theodore Mullens Pumpkin Smoothie

Preparation Time: 10 minutes

Servings: 2

Ingredients:

- 1 cup pumpkin puree
- ½ cup cranberries
- ½ cup raw cashews, soaked
- 2 small apples, chopped
- 1 orange, peeled and chopped
- 2 cups non-dairy milk
- ½ teaspoon cinnamon

- 4 tablespoons coconut milk
- 10 drops stevia

Preparation:

1. Add apples, orange, and pumpkin puree in a high speed blender. Blend well.
2. Now, add remaining ingredients and blend until a smooth mixture is formed.
3. Pour into serving glasses, serve, and enjoy!

Serving Suggestions: Top with apple slices before serving.

Variation Tip: You can use dairy milk instead of non-dairy milk.

Nutritional Information per Serving:

Calories: 583 | **Fat:** 27.4g|**Sat Fat:** 10.2g|**Carbohydrates:** 77.4g|**Fiber:** 15.2g|**Sugar:** 47.6g|**Protein:** 15.8g

Patrick Brewer Banana Coconut Smoothie

Preparation Time: 10 minutes

Servings: 2

Ingredients:

- 4 bananas
- 4 tablespoons coconut milk
- ½ cup shredded coconut
- ½ teaspoon vanilla essence
- 2 cups water

Preparation:

1. Add bananas, coconut milk, shredded coconut, vanilla essence and water in a blender. Blend well.
2. Take out and pour in the serving glasses.
3. Serve and enjoy!

Serving Suggestions: Top with banana slices before serving.

Variation Tip: You can also add cinnamon to enhance taste.

Nutritional Information per Serving:

Calories: 353 | **Fat:** 14.6g|**Sat Fat:** 12.5g|**Carbohydrates:** 58.7g|**Fiber:** 8.6g|**Sugar:** 31.2g|**Protein:** 3.9g

Johnny Rose Apple Smoothie

Preparation Time: 10 minutes

Servings: 4

Ingredients:

- 4 apples, chopped
- 2 cups water
- 1 teaspoon vanilla extract
- 1 teaspoon ground cinnamon
- A pinch of allspice

Preparation:

1. Add apples, water, vanilla extract, ground cinnamon, and allspice in a blender and blend until a smooth mixture is formed.
2. Take out and pour in serving glasses.
3. Serve and enjoy!

Serving Suggestions: Garnish with whipped cream before serving.

Variation Tip: You can add a little bit of protein powder to enhance taste.

Nutritional Information per Serving:

Calories: 121 | **Fat:** 0.4g|**Sat Fat:** 0g|**Carbohydrates:** 31.4g|**Fiber:** 5.7g|**Sugar:** 23.3g|**Protein:** 0.6g

Moira Rose Strawberry-Raspberry Smoothie

Preparation Time: 10 minutes

Servings: 2

Ingredients:

- 2 cups water

- 2 cups frozen strawberries
- 2 teaspoons raw honey
- 1 cup frozen raspberries

Preparation:

1. Add water, raspberries, honey, and strawberries in a food processor.
2. Pulse to form a smooth mixture.
3. Take out and serve.

Serving Suggestions: Top with raw raspberries and strawberries before serving.

Variation Tip: You can fresh raspberries and strawberries instead of frozen.

Nutritional Information per Serving:

Calories: 200 | **Fat:** 0.2g|**Sat Fat:** 0g|**Carbohydrates:** 51.5g|**Fiber:** 8.5g|**Sugar:** 41.9g|**Protein:** 0.9g

David Rose Guava Papaya Smoothie

Preparation Time: 10 minutes

Servings: 4

Ingredients:

- 4 cups papaya
- 4 guavas
- 2 cups ice cubes
- 4 teaspoons lemon juice
- 2 teaspoons ginger
- 3 teaspoons maple syrup

Preparation:

1. Add papaya and ginger in a blender. Blend well.
2. Now, add in guavas, ice cubes, lemon juice, and maple syrup. Blend until a smooth mixture is formed.
3. Take out and serve.

Serving Suggestions: You can serve with mint leaves.

Variation Tip: You can use stevia instead of maple syrup.

Nutritional Information per Serving:

Calories: 141 | **Fat:** 1.4g | **Sat Fat:** 0.4g | **Carbohydrates:** 32.7g | **Fiber:** 7.5g | **Sugar:** 22.5g | **Protein:** 3.1g

Chicken Recipes

Alexis Rose Bacon Wrapped Chicken Tenders

Preparation Time: 15 minutes
Cooking Time: 30 minutes

Servings: 2

Ingredients:

- 5 bacon strips, halved
- ¼ teaspoon onion powder
- ¼ tablespoon paprika
- ¼ teaspoon garlic powder
- 2 chicken breasts, skinless, sliced into strips
- Salt and pepper, to taste

Preparation:

1. Preheat the oven to 400 degrees F.
2. Add garlic powder, paprika, onion powder, salt, and pepper in a bowl. Mix well.
3. Add in chicken strips and toss them in the mixture to coat well.
4. Now, wrap each chicken strip with bacon and place them on the baking sheet and bake for about 30 minutes (15 minutes on each side).
5. Take out, serve and enjoy!

Serving Suggestions: Top with chopped mint leaves before serving.

Variation Tip: You can also use BBQ sauce to enhance taste.

Nutritional Information per Serving:

Calories: 521 | **Fat:** 33g|**Sat Fat:** 10.4g|**Carbohydrates:** 1g|**Fiber:** 0.4g|**Sugar:** 0.3g|**Protein:** 50.7g

Jocelyn Schitt African Style Chicken Stew

Preparation Time: 15 minutes
Cooking Time: 8 hours 5 minutes

Servings: 2

Ingredients:

- 2 pounds chicken pieces
- ½ teaspoon dried thyme
- 2 tomatoes, chopped
- ½ teaspoon paprika
- 2 carrots, sliced
- ¼ teaspoon cumin powder
- ¼ cup tomato sauce
- 1½ garlic cloves, minced
- ¼ cup chicken stock
- ½ cup oil
- Salt and pepper, to taste

Preparation:

1. Add oil in a skillet and place it over high heat.
2. Meanwhile, season chicken with salt and pepper.
3. Add chicken in oil and cook for 2 minutes on each side.
4. Now, transfer chicken in slow cooker and add remaining ingredients in it.
5. Mix well and close the lid.
6. Cook for about 8 hours and take out.
7. Serve and enjoy!

Serving Suggestions: Top with chopped cilantro before serving.

Variation Tip: Use chili sauce instead of tomato sauce.

Nutritional Information per Serving:

Calories: 1415 | **Fat:** 88.7g|**Sat Fat:** 16.4g|**Carbohydrates:** 15.9g|**Fiber:** 3.9g|**Sugar:** 7.8g|**Protein:** 134g

Mutt Schitt Roasted Dried Herb Drumsticks

Preparation Time: 10 minutes
Cooking Time: 50 minutes

Servings: 2

Ingredients:

- 1 pound chicken drumsticks
- 1 teaspoon dried oregano
- ½ teaspoon dried basil
- 2 tablespoons olive oil
- ½ teaspoon garlic powder
- ½ teaspoon dried parsley
- ½ teaspoon onion powder
- ¼ teaspoon dried rosemary
- Salt and black pepper, to taste

Preparation:

1. Heat up the baking oven to 400 degrees F.
2. Marinade chicken with oil and spices. Set aside.
3. Arrange the chicken drumsticks on the baking sheet and bake for about 40 minutes.
4. Take out and serve.

Serving Suggestions: Serve with any sauce of your choice.

Variation Tip: Add red chili flakes to enhance taste.

Nutritional Information per Serving:

Calories: 511 | **Fat:** 27.1g|**Sat Fat:** 5.5g|**Carbohydrates:** 1.6g|**Fiber:** 0.5g|**Sugar:** 0.4g|**Protein:** 62.7g

Stevie Budd Pineapple Citrus Marinated Chicken

Preparation Time: 20 minutes
Cooking Time: 45 minutes

Servings: 8

Ingredients:

- 16 chicken drumsticks
- 1 teaspoon paprika
- 4 garlic cloves, minced
- 1 cup fresh lime juice
- ½ cup fresh oregano
- 1 cup orange juice
- 1 cup pineapple juice
- 1 teaspoon ground cumin
- ½ cup olive oil

Preparation:

1. Add chicken drumsticks, paprika, garlic cloves, lime juice, oregano, orange juice, pineapple juice, ground cumin, and olive oil in a large bowl and mix well.
2. Marinate the chicken and set aside for 12 hours.
3. Meanwhile, warm up the oven to 425 degrees F.
4. Place the chicken drumsticks on the baking dish and bake for about 45 minutes.
5. Take out and serve.

Serving Suggestions: Garnish with cilantro and lime wedges before serving.

Variation Tip: Use jalapeno for even better taste.

Nutritional Information per Serving:

Calories: 313 | **Fat:** 18.5g|**Sat Fat:** 3.3g|**Carbohydrates:** 11.4g|**Fiber:** 2.2g|**Sugar:** 6.1g|**Protein:** 26.3g

Roland Schitt BBQ Chicken Drumsticks

Preparation Time: 10 minutes
Cooking Time: 8 hours
Servings: 2

Ingredients:

- 6 chicken drumsticks
- 1 tablespoon apple cider vinegar

- 1 tablespoon red chili powder
- ½ cup BBQ sauce
- ½ teaspoon onion powder
- ½ tablespoon paprika
- ½ teaspoon garlic powder
- ¼ tablespoon ground cumin
- 2 tablespoons honey
- Salt and pepper, to taste

Preparation:

1. Add drumsticks, apple cider vinegar, chili powder, BBQ sauce, onion powder, paprika, garlic powder, ground cumin, salt, and pepper in a slow cooker. Mix properly.
2. Cover the lid of slow cooker and cook for about 8 hours.
3. Take out and pour honey on drumsticks.
4. Serve and enjoy!

Serving Suggestions: Serve with tortilla or bread.

Variation Tip: Replace red chili powder with red chili flakes.

Nutritional Information per Serving:

Calories: 417 | **Fat:** 9.1g|**Sat Fat:** 2.2g|**Carbohydrates:** 44.4g|**Fiber:** 2.5g|**Sugar:** 34.4g|**Protein:** 39.1g

Twyla Sands Basil Pesto Chicken

Preparation Time: 10 minutes
Cooking Time: 30 minutes

Servings: 2

Ingredients:

- 2 chicken breasts, skinless and boneless
- 1 cup fresh basil leaves
- 1½ garlic cloves, minced
- ¼ teaspoon red pepper flakes
- ¼ cup pine nuts
- ¼ cup olive oil

- Salt and black pepper, to taste

Preparation:

1. Preheat the oven to 375 degrees F.
2. Add basil, garlic, pine nuts, and pepper flakes in a food processor. Pulse well.
3. Add in olive oil and blend again.
4. Arrange chicken breasts on the baking sheet and pour basil pesto on it.
5. Bake for about 30 minutes and take out.
6. Serve and enjoy!

Serving Suggestions: Serve with chili sauce.

Variation Tip: Replace black pepper with white pepper.

Nutritional Information per Serving:

Calories: 612 | **Fat:** 47.4g|**Sat Fat:** 7.3g|**Carbohydrates:** 5.4g|**Fiber:** 1.1g|**Sugar:** 0.8g|**Protein:** 43.8g

Robert Currie Roasted Chicken Thighs

Preparation Time: 10 minutes
Cooking Time: 24 minutes

Servings: 2

Ingredients:

- 4 chicken thighs
- ¼ teaspoon garlic powder
- ½ teaspoon paprika
- ½ teaspoon dried oregano
- ½ teaspoon onion flakes
- Salt and black pepper, to taste

Preparation:

1. Preheat the oven to 375 degrees F.
2. Arrange chicken thighs in a baking dish and top them with garlic powder, paprika, oregano, onion flakes, salt, and pepper.
3. Bake for about 45 minutes and take out.
4. Serve and enjoy!

Serving Suggestions: Serve with some herbs.

Variation Tip: Use white pepper instead of black pepper.

Nutritional Information per Serving:

Calories: 537 | **Fat:** 20.9g | **Sat Fat:** 5.7g | **Carbohydrates:** 1.2g | **Fiber:** 0.4g | **Sugar:** 0.3g | **Protein:** 81.2g

Veronica Lee Chicken Piccata

Preparation Time: 15 minutes
Cooking Time: 30 minutes

Servings: 8

Ingredients:

- 8 skinless chicken breasts
- 1 lemon, sliced
- 2 cups cassava flour
- 4 tablespoons ghee
- 4 tablespoons cooking oil
- ½ cup capers, rinsed
- 2 red onions, finely chopped
- 1 cup chicken stock
- 4 garlic cloves, crushed
- Salt and pepper, to taste

Preparation:

1. Add cassava flour, salt, and pepper in a bowl. Mix well.
2. Add chicken and toss to coat well.
3. Meanwhile, heat oil in a skillet and place chicken in it.
4. Transfer the chicken in a plate as soon as it becomes golden brown on both sides.
5. Now, add onion and garlic in a pan and cook for about 4 minutes.
6. Add in chicken stock and cook well.
7. Stir in lemon slices, capers, and butter.
8. Add chicken again in the pan and season with salt and pepper.
9. Cook for about 5 minutes and take out.
10. Serve and enjoy!

Serving Suggestions: Top with soy sauce and vinegar before serving.

Variation Tip: You can add spices of your choice.

Nutritional Information per Serving:

Calories: 486 | **Fat:** 24.1g | **Sat Fat:** 7.9g | **Carbohydrates:** 24.2g | **Fiber:** 4.1g | **Sugar:** 1.5g | **Protein:** 41.7g

Snacks Recipes

Theodore Mullens Roasted Peanuts

Preparation Time: 10 minutes
Cooking Time: 14 minutes

Servings: 6

Ingredients:

- 1 cup peanuts
- ½ tablespoon water
- ½ teaspoon olive oil
- 2 tablespoons unsweetened applesauce

- ¼ teaspoon ground cinnamon
- ½ tablespoon brown sugar
- Salt, to taste

Preparation:

1. Heat the oven to 350 degrees F.
2. Arrange peanuts on the baking sheet and roast for about 10 minutes.
3. Add applesauce, water, and oil in a bowl. Mix properly.
4. Add roasted peanuts in applesauce mixture and mix until peanuts are coated properly with the mixture.
5. Place peanuts again on the baking sheet and sprinkle ground cinnamon on them.
6. Bake for about 4 minutes and take out.
7. Serve and enjoy!

Serving Suggestions: Pour honey on the top before serving.

Variation Tip: Unsweetened applesauce can be replaced with maple syrup.

Nutritional Information per Serving:

Calories: 147 | **Fat:** 12.4g|**Sat Fat:** 1.7g|**Carbohydrates:** 5.3g| **Fiber:** 2.2g|**Sugar:** 2.2g|**Protein:** 6.3g

Patrick Brewer Cod Sticks

Preparation Time: 10 minutes
Cooking Time: 15 minutes

Servings: 8

Ingredients:

- 1 cup almond flour
- 2 teaspoon dried parsley, crushed
- 1 cod fillet, sliced thinly
- ½ teaspoon cayenne pepper
- 2 eggs
- Salt and black pepper, to taste

Preparation:

1. Warm up the baking oven to 350 degrees F.
2. Meanwhile, add eggs in a large bowl and whisk well.
3. Add almond flour, parsley, cayenne pepper, salt, and pepper in another bowl. Mix well.
4. Dip cod fillet slices in whisked eggs and then dip them in flour mixture.
5. Arrange them on greased baking dish and bake for about 6 minutes on each side.
6. Take out and serve.

Serving Suggestions: Serve with red chili sauce.

Variation Tip: Replace almond flour with coconut flour.

Nutritional Information per Serving:

Calories: 111 | **Fat:** 7.9g|**Sat Fat:** 0.8g|**Carbohydrates:** 3.2g|**Fiber:** 1.5g|**Sugar:** 0.1g|**Protein:** 6.9g

Johnny Rose Cheddar Biscuits

Preparation Time: 15 minutes
Cooking Time: 15 minutes

Servings: 8

Ingredients:

- 4 eggs
- ¼ teaspoon baking powder
- ¼ cup melted butter
- ¼ cup coconut flour, sifted
- 1/8 teaspoon garlic powder
- 1/8 teaspoon ginger powder
- 1 cup cheddar cheese
- 1 teaspoon chopped mint leaves

Preparation:

1. Preheat the oven to 400 degrees F.
2. Line a cookie sheet with greased foil paper.
3. Meanwhile, add flour, baking powder, garlic powder, and salt in a large bowl. Mix well.
4. Add eggs and butter in another bowl. Beat well.
5. Combine the two mixtures and add cheese. Mix properly.
6. Pour the batter in the cookie sheet and bake for about 15 minutes.
7. Take out, serve and enjoy!

Serving Suggestions: Serve with chopped mint leaves on the top.

Variation Tip: You can also use almond flour.

Nutritional Information per Serving:

Calories: 155 | **Fat:** 13g|**Sat Fat:** 7.6g|**Carbohydrates:** 3g|**Fiber:** 1.5g|**Sugar:** 0.3g|**Protein:** 6.9g

Moira Rose Spicy Cashews

Preparation Time: 15 minutes
Cooking Time: 2 hours 40 minutes

Servings: 24

Ingredients:

- 5 cups cashews
- 3 tablespoons butter
- 6 tablespoons chili seasoning mix

Preparation:

1. Add cashews, chili seasoning mix, and butter in a slow cooker. Mix well.
2. Cover the lid and cook for about 2 hours 30 minutes on low heat.
3. Open the lid and stir properly.
4. Cook for 15 minutes and take out.
5. Serve and enjoy!

Serving Suggestions: Serve with red chili flakes on the top.

Variation Tip: You can replace butter with olive oil.

Nutritional Information per Serving:

Calories: 182 | **Fat:** 15g | **Sat Fat:** 3.6g | **Carbohydrates:** 10.4g | **Fiber:** 1.5g | **Sugar:** 1.6g | **Protein:** 4.6g

David Rose Chickpea Crackers

Preparation Time: 30 minutes
Cooking Time: 20 minutes

Servings: 10

Ingredients:

- 1 cup chickpea flour
- ½ teaspoon baking powder
- 2 tablespoons nutritional yeast
- 2 teaspoons toasted sesame seeds
- ½ cup water
- ¼ teaspoon turmeric
- ½ teaspoon sesame oil
- Salt, to taste

Preparation:

1. Preheat the oven to 350 degrees F.
2. Meanwhile, add chickpea flour, baking powder, yeast, sesame seeds, turmeric, and salt in a large bowl. Mix well.
3. Add oil and water gradually in the mixture and mix well until proper dough is formed.
4. Cover the dough until it rises.
5. Now, dust the surface and press the dough with tortilla press.
6. Put the pressed dough on the non-stick cookie sheet and bake for about 20 minutes.
7. Take out and serve.

Serving Suggestions: Serve with mayo dip or any sauce of your choice.

Variation Tip: You can add olive oil instead of sesame oil.

Nutritional Information per Serving:

Calories: 86 | **Fat:** 1.9g|**Sat Fat:** 0.2g|**Carbohydrates:** 13.4g|**Fiber:** 4.1g|**Sugar:** 2.1g|**Protein:** 4.9g

Alexis Rose Herb Crackers

Preparation Time: 25 minutes
Cooking Time: 20 minutes

Servings: 8

Ingredients:

- 1 cup almond flour
- 1 tablespoon herbes de provence
- 1 tablespoon water
- ½ tablespoon olive oil
- Salt, to taste

Preparation:

1. Add almond flour, herbes de provence, and salt in a large bowl. Mix well.
2. Now, add in olive oil and water. Whisk properly until soft dough is formed.
3. Make small spheres out of the dough and press them with tortilla press.
4. Place them on the baking sheet lined with parchment paper.
5. Bake in the oven already heated at 350 degrees F for about 20 minutes.
6. Take out and serve.

Serving Suggestions: Serve with garlic mayo sauce.

Variation Tip: You can use almond oil.

Nutritional Information per Serving:

Calories: 154 | **Fat:** 12.6g | **Sat Fat:** 1.3g | **Carbohydrates:** 3.5g | **Fiber:** 4g | **Sugar:** 0.4g | **Protein:** 6.8g

Jocelyn Schitt Lemon Scones

Preparation Time: 15 minutes
Cooking Time: 25 minutes

Servings: 6

Ingredients:

- 1½ cups all-purpose flour
- 1 teaspoon lemon extract
- ½ cup unsweetened soy milk
- 1 tablespoon sunflower oil
- ¼ cup sugar
- 1 tablespoon baking powder
- Salt, to taste

Preparation:

1. Preheat the oven to 400 degrees F.
2. Add dry ingredients in one bowl and wet in another. Mix properly.
3. Combine the two mixtures, mix to form a dough, and make small spheres out of it.
4. Press with tortilla press and make any shape you want.
5. Place scones on the cookie sheet and bake for about 15 minutes.
6. Take out and serve.

Serving Suggestions: Serve with maple syrup.

Variation Tip: All-purpose flour can be replaced with almond flour.

Nutritional Information per Serving:

Calories: 484 | **Fat:** 3.8g|**Sat Fat:** 0.5g|**Carbohydrates:** 98.3g|**Fiber:** 3.3g|**Sugar:** 9.5g|**Protein:** 12.5g

Mutt Schitt Banana Biscuits

Preparation Time: 25 minutes
Cooking Time: 30 minutes

Servings: 15

Ingredients:

- 2 bananas, peeled and mashed
- ½ tablespoon baking powder
- ½ cup soy milk
- 2¼ cups white flour
- 1 tablespoon canola oil

Preparation:

1. Heat the oven to 425 degrees F.
2. Mash bananas in a bowl and add soymilk, and oil. Mix well.

3. Now, add baking powder and flour. Stir well.
4. Knead the dough and roll it with the help of rolling pin.
5. Cut into circles and place on the greased cookie sheet.
6. Bake for about 20 minutes and take out.
7. Serve and enjoy!

Serving Suggestions: Enjoy with tea.

Variation Tip: Use canola oil instead of olive oil.

Nutritional Information per Serving:

Calories: 186 | **Fat:** 1.6g|**Sat Fat:** 0.2g|**Carbohydrates:** 37.7g|**Fiber:** 1.7g|**Sugar:** 2.4g|**Protein:** 5g

Dessert Recipes

Stevie Budd Blueberry Ice-cream

Preparation Time: 15 minutes

Servings: 2

Ingredients:

- ½ cup fresh blueberries
- ¼ cup coconut cream
- 1 tablespoon shredded coconut
- ½ cup fresh raspberries

Preparation:

1. Add blueberries, raspberries, coconut cream, and shredded coconut in a food processor and pulse until a smooth mixture is formed.
2. Transfer the mixture in an ice-cream maker and process according to manufacturer's directions.
3. Pour the mixture in an air-tight container and freeze it for about 4 hours.
4. Take out and serve.

Serving Suggestions: Pour blueberry syrup on ice-cream before serving.

Variation Tip: Replace coconut cream with fresh cream.

Nutritional Information per Serving:

Calories: 115 | **Fat:** 8.3g|**Sat Fat:** 7.1g|**Carbohydrates:** 11g|**Fiber:** 3.8g|**Sugar:** 6.1g|**Protein:** 1.4g

Roland Schitt Chickpea Fudge

Preparation Time: 10 minutes
Cooking Time: 1 hour

Servings: 3

Ingredients:

- ½ cup cooked chickpeas
- ¼ teaspoon vanilla extract
- 2 tablespoons almond butter
- 2 dates, pitted and chopped
- ½ tablespoon cocoa powder
- ½ cup almond milk

Preparation:

1. Add almond milk, almond butter, dates, chickpeas, vanilla extract in a blender. Blend well.
2. Transfer the mixture in a bowl and add cocoa powder in it.
3. Mix well and pour the batter in a parchment paper lined baking sheet.
4. Set the mixture on the surface and bake for about 1 hour.
5. Take out and refrigerate.
6. Serve and enjoy!

Serving Suggestions: Serve with chocolate chips on the top.

Variation Tip: Replace almond milk with coconut milk.

Nutritional Information per Serving:

Calories: 297 | **Fat:** 17.7g|**Sat Fat:** 9.2g|**Carbohydrates:** 29.1g|**Fiber:** 8.5g|**Sugar:** 8.9g|**Protein:** 9.9g

Twyla Sands Blackberry Crumble

Preparation Time: 10 minutes
Cooking Time: 45 minutes

Servings: 4

Ingredients:

- ¼ cup coconut flour
- ½ tablespoon fresh lemon juice
- ¼ cup banana, peeled and mashed
- 2 tablespoons melted butter
- 3 tablespoons water
- 1 teaspoon baking soda
- 1½ cups fresh blackberries
- ¼ cup arrowroot flour

Preparation:

1. Warm up the oven to 300 degrees F and oil a baking dish.
2. Meanwhile, add arrowroot flour, baking soda, water, melted butter, banana, coconut flour, and fresh lime juice in a large bowl. Mix well.
3. Now, arrange blackberries in a baking dish and pour the batter on them.
4. Bake for about 40 minutes and take out.
5. Serve and enjoy!

Serving Suggestions: Before serving, garnish with blackberries.

Variation Tip: You can also use blueberries to enhance taste.

Nutritional Information per Serving:

Calories: 180 | **Fat:** 7.6g|**Sat Fat:** 4.2g|**Carbohydrates:** 27.2g|**Fiber:** 13.8g|**Sugar:** 10.9g|**Protein:** 4.3g

Robert Currie Chocolate Mousse

Preparation Time: 20 minutes

Servings: 4

Ingredients:

- 2 teaspoons cocoa powder
- ½ cup tofu, drained
- 2 teaspoons almonds, chopped
- 1 teaspoon chocolate syrup

Preparation:

1. Add cocoa powder, tofu, almonds, and chocolate syrup in a blender. Blend well.
2. Pour the mixture in serving glasses and refrigerate.
3. Top with cream and serve.

Serving Suggestions: Top with some nuts and serve.

Variation Tip: You can use chocolate chips to enhance taste.

Nutritional Information per Serving:

Calories: 34 | **Fat:** 2g|**Sat Fat:** 0.4g|**Carbohydrates:** 2.3g|**Fiber:** 0.7g|**Sugar:** 1g|**Protein:** 3g

Veronica Lee Banana Custard

Preparation Time: 10 minutes
Cooking Time: 25 minutes

Servings: 4

Ingredients:

- 1 banana, peeled and finely mashed
- 1 egg
- ¼ teaspoon vanilla extract
- 1 cup almond milk

Preparation:

1. Heat up the baking oven to 350 degrees F and place lightly greased custard glasses in the baking dish.
2. Add banana, egg, vanilla extract, and almond milk in a bowl. Mix well.
3. Pour the mixture in custard glasses and add water in the baking dish.
4. Bake for about 25 minutes and take out.
5. Serve and enjoy!

Serving Suggestions: Top with some banana slices.

Variation Tip: You can use fresh dairy milk.

Nutritional Information per Serving:

Calories: 181 | **Fat:** 15.5g|**Sat Fat:** 13.1g|**Carbohydrates:** 10.2g|**Fiber:** 2.1g|**Sugar:** 5.7g|**Protein:** 3.1g

Theodore Mullens Blueberry Pudding

Preparation Time: 10 minutes
Servings: 3

Ingredients:

- 1 cup frozen blueberries
- 5 tablespoons water
- 1 teaspoon lime zest, grated finely
- 2 tablespoons fresh lime juice
- 10 drops liquid stevia

Preparation:

1. Add frozen blueberries, water, lime zest, lime juice, and stevia in a blender. Blend well.
2. Take out and top with blueberries.
3. Serve and enjoy!

Serving Suggestions: Enjoy with blueberry syrup on the top.

Variation Tip: You can also use honey or maple syrup to enhance taste.

Nutritional Information per Serving:

Calories: 35 | **Fat:** 0.2g|**Sat Fat:** 0g|**Carbohydrates:** 9.6g|**Fiber:** 1.4g|**Sugar:** 5.3g|**Protein:** 0.5g

Patrick Brewer Chocolate Custard

Preparation Time: 5 minutes
Cooking Time: 15 minutes

Servings: 3

Ingredients:

- 1 cup milk
- 1 egg
- 1½ tablespoons cocoa powder
- ½ tablespoon corn flour
- 2 tablespoons caster sugar

Preparation:

1. Heat milk in a non-stick pan.
2. Meanwhile, add egg, cocoa powder, corn flour, and sugar in a bowl. Sift properly.
3. Pour the mixture in hot milk and cook until the mixture thickens.
4. Take out and serve.

Serving Suggestions: Top with chocolate chips and serve.

Variation Tip: You can add some chocolate syrup to enhance taste.

Nutritional Information per Serving:

Calories: 118 | **Fat:** 4.5g|**Sat Fat:** 2.2g|**Carbohydrates:** 18.5g|**Fiber:** 3g|**Sugar:** 12g|**Protein:** 6.4g

Johnny Rose Mint Chocolate Chip Ice-cream

Preparation Time: 15 minutes

Servings: 5

Ingredients:

- ½ cup milk

- ½ cup chocolate chips
- ½ cup granulated sugar
- 1 cup heavy cream, well chilled
- 1 tablespoon pure peppermint extract

Preparation:

1. Add milk and sugar in a large bowl. Whisk well.
2. Now, add heavy cream and peppermint. Mix well.
3. Pour the mixture in an ice-cream maker and process according to manufacturer's directions.
4. Transfer the mixture in an airtight container and add chocolate chips in it.
5. Place the container in a freezer and take out after at least 2 hours.
6. Serve and enjoy!

Serving Suggestions: You can top it with mint leaves.

Variation Tip: White chocolate chips can also be used.

Nutritional Information per Serving:

Calories: 260 | **Fat:** 14.4g|**Sat Fat:** 9.3g|**Carbohydrates:** 31.9g|**Fiber:** 0.6g|**Sugar:** 29.8g|**Protein:** 2.6g

Conclusion

The book, Schitt's Creek Unofficial Cookbook is highly inspired by the famous comedy TV series known as Schitt's Creek. The book combines the idea of humour and food together by serving you the most delicious and nutritious recipes for every occasion. All the recipes come with easily understandable instructions and will change your entire approach towards food and life altogether.

Made in the USA
Columbia, SC
15 August 2021

43647613R00052